My Family Plays Music

by JUDY COX

illustrated by ELBRITE BROWN

Holiday House / New York

Library of Congress Cataloging-in-Publication Data

Cox, Judy.

My family plays music/by Judy Cox;

illustrated by Elbrite Brown—1st ed.

p.   cm.

Summary: A musical family with talents for playing a variety
of instruments enjoys getting together to celebrate.

ISBN 0-8234-1591-0 (hardcover)

[1. Musicians—Fiction. 2. Musical instruments—Fiction.

3. Family life—Fiction.] I. Brown, Elbrite, ill. II. Title.

PZ7.C83835 My 2001   00-044903

[E]—dc21

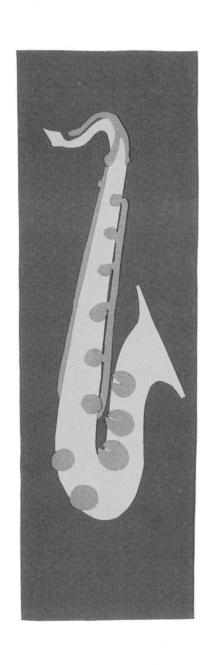

This is my family. We all love music.

This is my mom.
She plays fiddle in a country-and-western band.
She plays in honky-tonks and sings sad songs
about broken hearts while people dance real slow.
When I play with her, I play the tambourine.

This is my dad.
He plays cello in a string quartet.
He sits onstage at Symphony Hall
in a black tailcoat and a white bow tie.
When I play with him, I play the triangle.

This is my sister, Emily.
She plays clarinet in the marching band.
We cheer and wave as she struts down
Main Street in the big parade.
When I play with her, I play the cymbals.

LAKEWOOD MEDIA CENTER
HOLLAND, MI 49424

This is my brother, Paul.
He plays lead guitar in a rock 'n' roll band.
He wiggles and he spins and he shakes when
he plays for the dance in the high school gym.
When I play with him, I play the cowbell.

This is my aunt Saffron.
She plays vibes in a jazz combo.
She plays soft, cool sounds at the Blue Note Club.
Her hands dance the mallets up and down
the bars—*pung, pong, ping.*
When I play with her, I play the woodblock.

This is my uncle Woody.
He plays saxophone in a big band.
He blows swing tunes at the Paragon Ballroom
while dancers glide beneath the flashing mirror ball.
When I play with him, I play the maracas.

This is my grandma.
She plays banjo in a bluegrass band.
She picks mountain melodies for folks who sit
on folding chairs and tap their toes to the spunky beat.
When I play with her, I play the jug.

This is my grandpa.
He plays tuba in a polka band.
He dresses in lederhosen and a hat with a feather.
His cheeks puff out round and red
as he blows oompah-pah, oompah-pah.
When I play with him, I play rhythm sticks.

This is my great-grandmother.
She plays the pipe organ in St. Peter's Cathedral.
On Sunday morning we sit straight and still
as she pumps out music
that swells likes waves.
When I play with her, I play the handbell.

This is my cousin, Dean.
He plays bongos at the Full Ear Cafe.
He slips his drums between his knees and raps
and pats them with his hands,
keeping the beat while people recite
poems that don't rhyme.
When I play with him, I play wind chimes.

This is my niece, Sadie.
She plays pots and pans, drumming on them
with a wooden spoon.
She plays LOUD!
When I play with her, I play the big soup kettle.

This is me. I play tambourine, triangle, cymbals,
cowbell, woodblock, maracas, rhythm sticks,
handbell, wind chimes, and soup kettle.
Daddy says I'm a percussionist.

This is my family.
We all love different kinds of music,
but we all love one another.
And when we get together, we celebrate!

GLOSSARY

Big band Big bands, like orchestras, use brass and woodwind instruments. Unlike orchestras, they do not use strings. Instead they add other popular instruments such as piano, saxophone, electric guitar, and electric bass. There is also a drummer who plays a set of drums with cymbals attached to it. Big bands reached their heyday in the 1940s, playing in dance halls and public ballrooms.

Bluegrass Bluegrass is a type of traditional country music. It is played on folk instruments such as mandolins, banjos, acoustic guitars, dulcimers, harmonicas, and fiddles.

Brass Brass instruments produce sound when the player's lips vibrate against the mouth-piece of the horn. Brass instruments include trumpets, tubas, trombones, and French horns.

Country-and-western Country-and-western has its roots in rural southern folk music. Country-and-western music is traditionally played by a combo of bass guitar, drums, electric and acoustic guitars, steel guitar, and fiddle. The lyrics often tell a story.

Honky-tonk A dance hall where country-and-western music is played.

Jazz Jazz developed in America in about 1900. It is based on blues songs, which are based on African slave songs, and uses African rhythms and Western instruments and harmonies. Jazz has melodies, words, and rhythms that are often made up on the spot or improvised. A jazz song changes a little each time it is played and seldom sounds the same twice.

Marching band Marching bands use brass, woodwind, and percussion instruments. Traditionally formed as military bands, they now also entertain at football games and parades. In addition to playing instruments, marching band members must also learn to march in formation.

Percussion Percussion instruments are shaken, struck, or hit. They make the bangs, bongs, and crashes in music. They include drums of all sorts, cymbals big and small, tambourines, triangles, bells, wind chimes, and also vibes and xylophones (because they are played with mallets).

Polka Polka bands play polkas, schottisches, and waltzes. They use brass and woodwind instruments, such as clarinets, cornets, and trombones, and often add a small drum set and button box accordion. Polka bands originated to play the polka, a hopping, twirling dance from Bohemia. Now polka bands

play at weddings, festivals, and dances all over the country.

Rock 'n' roll Rock 'n' roll began in the 1950s from a combination of blues and country. Rock 'n' roll songs usually combine a strong beat with an uncomplicated melody. Rock 'n' roll bands use a drum set, electric guitars, and electric basses. They may add an electric piano, organ, or synthesizer.

String quartet A small music ensemble consisting of two violins, cello, and viola. String quartets play chamber music, a type of classical music in which each instrument plays a different part.

Strings Stringed instruments produce sound when the strings vibrate. Strings can be played by plucking, as on a banjo; strumming, as on a guitar; hammering, as on a piano; or bowing, as on a violin. Stringed instruments also include harp, viola, cello, and mandolin.

Woodwind Woodwind instruments are played by blowing air across a hole, such as in a flute, or into a mouthpiece to vibrate the reeds attached to it, such as in a saxophone. Woodwinds are not always made of wood, just as brass instruments are not always made of brass. Woodwinds also include clarinet, oboe, and bassoon.

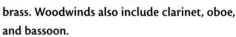